For Daisy

ACKNOWLEDGEMENTS

The author and publisher are grateful to the following for supplying and authorizing reproduction of the illustrations. If any copyright owner has unwittingly been overlooked the publishers will be glad to rectify this in future editions.

(The letters at the end of each caption indicate the source of the photographs.)

(H) BBC Hulton Picture Library.
(F) Flashbacks.
(KY) Keystone Press Agency Ltd.
(K) The Kobal Collection.
(PA) The Press Association.
(R) Rex Features Ltd. ((RB): photograph by Gianni Bozzacchi © Forum.)
(SC) Scope Features.
(S) Syndication International Ltd.

The photographs (by Brian Moody) on the title page and on page 4 are reproduced by permission of Scope Features. The photographs on page 83 and 94 (RB) are from Rex Features.

Jacket/cover: The photograph of Richard Burton on the front is from *Exorcist II: The Heretic* (1977) and is reproduced by permission of Flashbacks.
On the back the photograph top left is from *The Robe* (1953) and is reproduced by permission of Flashbacks. The three remaining photographs are reproduced by permission of Syndication International Ltd.

CONTENTS

A star goes home: fresh from his early success in Hollywood, Richard Burton returns to the village of Pontrhydyfen. With him is his wife Sybil and brother Ivor. The house where he was born is in the row at the foot of the hill. (H)

I
AN ENVIABLE MAN

THE FAMOUS are not always happy. They have to live, not only with themselves, but with our distorted picture of their brilliance, their wit, their beauty or their skill. Richard Burton had to live with the legend of his greatness as an actor, his prowess in taking women to bed, his weakness for alcohol and his marriages to Elizabeth Taylor – who is a legend of her own. He had to live with the expectations of others, expectations that were never quite realized. But it was different once.

His heyday as far as the world was concerned came with the fame that followed his public courtship of Taylor, the films they made together, and their marriage. For fifteen years, from the early 1960s, Burton and Taylor were an endless source of gossip, scandal and sexual excitement.

His real heyday, when he had tasted success but not the bitterness that can go with it, came earlier, years before Elizabeth Taylor invaded his life.

In 1955, Richard Burton was thirty years old. Born Richard Walter Jenkins, tenth child of a Welsh coal miner who drank too much, he was making two parallel careers for himself. In London he was the most talked about young stage actor of his generation, playing classic Shakespearian roles with an arrogance that was almost disdain. In Hollywood he was a film star who had appeared alongside Olivia de Havilland in *My Cousin Rachel* and Jean Simmons in *The Robe*, a Biblical spectacular, filmed (as often happened in those days) on a man-made Palestinian hillside in the middle of Los Angeles.

Young Burton, already a rich man beyond the expectations of someone from his lowly background, seemed able to take both careers in his stride.

He was not the dedicated theatre actor, nose to the grindstone, prepared to put up with modest rewards for the sake of his craft. He acted casually, as though by instinct, his fine head and broad shoulders commanding attention in an odd way, even when he was silent, that fascinated audiences.

Nor was he one of the run-of-the-mill young leading men in Hollywood, making prepared remarks for publicists, all smiles and emptiness, as they were apt to be then. He was a bit of a tearaway, a funny Welshman who claimed to know six hundred songs in Welsh, and even sang some of them at parties in Beverly Hills.

He made odd, unfilmstar-like remarks. The studio had given him a Cadillac, but he didn't know what to do with it. Success alarmed him. His family back in

Wales didn't know what to make of it all, he said, and neither did he. He added that the Californian sunlight was too much for him.

He pulled the legs of reporters. Always quick to say that the Jenkins family had been dismally poor in its Glamorganshire village when he was young – which was true – he added ludicrous details. He said the entire family once lived for eight months on the equivalent of a dollar. Somebody wrote it down and printed it. Who could tell what was true when it fell from the lips of this wicked Welshman with the devastating voice?

Somewhere between the roles of classic actor and mischievous filmstar, Burton moved confidently from one success to the next. When first he left to make films in California, at the age of twenty-six, admirers feared that the British theatre, where he earned a modest salary like everyone else, had lost him to the fleshpots. But a year later, after *The Robe* and other pictures, he was back for a Shakespeare season at the Old Vic, playing Hamlet for the first time, at fifty pounds a week. Again he was acclaimed. Again he returned to Hollywood, this time to make pictures that included *The Rains of Ranchipur*, a remake of the famous 1939 movie, *The Rains Came*.

His co-star was Lana Turner. When the draft script came into the studio, the producer wrote 'More sex' on it. More sex or no, the film was unmemorable. But for a few weeks' work, Burton earned the equivalent of twenty years' salary as an Old Vic actor.

Then in 1955, for the second time, he returned to London and the theatre. He was becoming a stage-and-cinema commuter, nicely balancing the two halves of his career.

On his thirtieth birthday in November, he was preparing to begin a new Shakespeare season with the part of Henry V. He was heard to remark that he was getting tired of the great classical roles. 'I want to be in a play where I can smoke a cigarette,' he said. But this was taken to be another of Richard's jokes.

He was a man with his feet on the ground. His wife was a silver-haired Welsh girl called Sybil. His family were fond of her, and they, like she, helped to anchor his life in the proud but modest working-class background from which he came. His brothers and sisters travelled up by train from Port Talbot to see him act in Shakespeare, the men in the dinner jackets they wore to sing in choirs, the women in floral silks.

Cecilia, or 'Cissie,' the sister who brought him up when his mother died, was at the Old Vic to see him play Iago in *Othello*. She loved her brother fiercely. Her only word of reproach was that when his photograph appeared in the papers, he sometimes wore a polo-neck pullover.

'Put on a white shirt and a collar and tie, there's a good boy,' she told him. 'It's so much nicer.' He teased her by offering her champagne in the dressing room; she tightened her lips and said nothing. After the performance she was in tears. 'Rich, Rich,' she said, 'if only Mam could have seen you!'

If the family knew or suspected that he sometimes drank like a fish, and found it hard to keep his hands off the ladies, they kept their thoughts to themselves. A friend from Burton's schooldays was invited to see him in Hamlet, and met a brother or two in a pub opposite Waterloo Station, just down the road from the Old Vic. They were all boisterous together, noisy Welshmen crowded up at the bar, but underneath was a hint of nervousness.

In Burton's dressing room he introduced them to his Ophelia, Claire Bloom. Sybil was there, and the school friend sensed the tension between her and the very young and beautiful Miss Bloom. Although Sybil, from the start of her marriage, had given her husband a long rein, in this instance she warned him lest he allow his feelings for Miss Bloom to develop into something stronger than admiration.

Despite everything, there was an air of reliability about Burton. In the eyes of his family he was kind and amusing, and in a strange way unchanged by what had happened. The cosmopolitan actor still arrived in the mining valley (in his Jaguar) wearing an old jacket, spent an evening in the Miners Arms telling them scurrilous stories about Hollywood and how farcical the film business was, and ended up at one of his brothers' little houses, eating eggs, bacon, peas and potatoes and drinking strong cups of tea.

Richard Burton at thirty seemed an enviable man. He was both 'showbiz star' and 'serious actor.' The London theatre critics continued to praise him. 'Within this actor,' wrote Kenneth Tynan, 'there is always something reserved, a secret upon which trespassers will be prosecuted, a rooted solitude which his Welsh blood tinges with mystery. Inside these limits, he is a master.'

Tynan added: 'Beyond them, he has much to learn.' But Burton had many years in which to do the learning, or so it seemed then. For the moment, he lived up to people's expectations. He was richly gifted. He had the knack of shaping life to him, instead of being at its mercy. 'I am the most placid actor in the business,' he said. He may even have been happy.

2
THE ACTOR FROM WALES

RICHARD BURTON was born on 10 November 1925, the year before the General Strike. The family lived in the mining village of Pontrhydyfen, which translates roughly into English as 'Cartersford Bridge.'

It was a district of copper works and shallow coal mines. The shafts went into the sides of hills from the top of which a collier and his sweetheart, lying in the bracken, could look to the southwest and see the round glare of Swansea Bay half a dozen miles away.

The Jenkinses lived in a cramped little row of houses called Dan-y-Bont, 'Under the Bridge.' They all spoke Welsh and English, but Welsh was the 'language of the hearth.'

Before the Industrial Revolution Burton's ancestors lived in the Vale of Glamorgan, between the coast and the hills. His great great grandfather, Miles Jenkins, was a cattle dealer; his great grandfather became a miller, and ground corn for the new industrial population in the valley around Pontrhydyfen. His grandfather and father were miners in the village, and it was in this tradition that Richard Jenkins could expect to find a living when the time came.

His mother was forty-two years old when he was born. Married at seventeen into a ravaging life of washdays, baking days and pregnancies, she had once been a tall, pretty blonde. At forty-four, after giving birth to one more child, she died of postnatal complications.

The children had to be farmed out among relatives. Richard, not yet two years old, went to his sister Cecilia, who was twenty years older and had recently married a miner. They lived a few miles away on the coast in Port Talbot, an austere steel town where smoke and rain clouds make the only castles in the air.

There, as in Pontrhydyfen, the future for a boy like Jenkins was likely to be the brutal labour of the pits, with its filth and wet and danger, or to be half roasted in front of a blast furnace. If he was lucky he might end up a clerk; if he was very lucky, he might find himself with a piece of chalk in his hand, teaching arithmetic.

Being an intelligent boy with character, he made some progress in the right direction, and reached Port Talbot Secondary School at the age of eleven. There he was mischievous, popular with other boys, and acted in a school play. The English master, a precise and clever bachelor called Burton, produced it. After four years, though, with money short at home, and no sign that Jenkins was going to be the 'brilliant scholar' that the Welsh respect so much, he was taken away from school and put to work behind the counter of the local Co-operative Stores.

It was 1941, the middle of the war. The gawky youth with acne in Men's Outfitting was not promising material as a haberdasher. Sometimes, instead of going home at midday, he slipped across the road to the Rugby Club, persuaded the barmaid to serve a cheeky lad of fifteen, and returned to the shop with beer on his breath. When one of his former teachers looked in at the Co-op, the manager said, 'What was he like in school? Because he's bloody hopeless here.'

Socks and underpants were beneath his dignity. He was a bit of a lad, a bit of a devil. Something burned in him. He liked boxing and singing. A teacher from his junior school ran a youth club, and young Jenkins was often there, lounging, strutting, laughing.

Schoolmasters are eternal optimists, always hoping to spot a thoroughbred among the donkeys. The idea took shape that Jenkins was worth saving. P.H. Burton, the English master, was one of the fixers behind the scenes. The school Governors were persuaded to take him back, a year and a half after he had left. The headmaster himself wasn't keen.

Jenkins had no family background to speak for him, no academic record, no influential friends. It is one of those mysterious episodes that sometimes occur in the early lives of men who are on the way to a fame undreamed of at the time: as though a hidden hand were at work, shaping destinies behind the scenes.

Perhaps the hidden hand was merely P.H. Burton. The stout, strict schoolmaster had an eye for boys with talent and good looks. He usually had someone in tow, grooming him for parts in school plays. 'P.H.' himself was a miner's son, but his parents were English, their home, in another valley, more genteel. The theatre fascinated him. He longed to make his name in it, writing and acting. But although he did both with competence, he knew he lacked the real fire. Thus he projected his longings – and eased the loneliness of a bachelor who lived in lodgings – by picking out surrogate sons from his pupils.

Richard Jenkins was the last of the line, the justification for the rest. One predecessor, a boy called Owen Jones, had won a scholarship to drama school in London, and appeared on the West End stage as Laertes to Laurence Olivier's Hamlet. Now Jones was in the armed forces. By 1943 he was dead.

Philip Burton put all his hopes on Richard Jenkins. The schoolmaster was thirty-eight; his own dreams of fame had receded. He found the boy a room in his lodgings and took over his upbringing. Cecilia hated to let him go, but her husband and Richard couldn't stand one another, and Richard's brother-in-law was glad to see the back of him; it was one mouth less to feed.

In the next year and a half, P.H. Burton gave his pupil a background. He crammed him for the school-leaving examination; bought him clothes; improved

Opposite above With his father, known locally as 'Dic Bach', 'Little Dick', a hard-drinking miner. They are crossing the 'Big Bridge' that spans the river at Pontrhydyfen. Hilda, one of Burton's sisters, still lives in the row of houses by Dic Bach's cap. (H)

The village Burton came from lived by coal. As a child, Burton assumed that, like his brothers, he would join the ranks of cloth-capped miners. When he returned to drink pints with his father and workmates, he mixed easily enough. But his new life in London and Hollywood made him like a man come back from another planet. (H)

Right Steel works and little 'two up, two down' houses were part of Burton's childhood. Life in South Wales gave him warm memories that he delighted to look back on. But part of him knew that once he had tasted success, he would never be at ease with the 'starved life' of the valleys. (H)

his manners; excited him with poetry; taught him to speak with less of an accent and more precision; told him about stagecraft; gave him his name.

If 'P.H.' had been three weeks older, he could have adopted him, and would have done. As it was, the difference between their ages was just too small to make adoption legally possible. Instead, Richard was made his ward until the age of twenty-one, and assumed the older man's name. There were some grumblings in the family: what was wrong with a good Welsh name like Jenkins? But Philip Burton was too forceful for them.

The papers were taken to Richard's real father to sign. By this time, the end of 1943, he was a lost soul, living in squalor near the docks in Cardiff. He didn't seem to know which son he was signing away.

The schoolmaster's strategy unfolded like a battle plan. He was commandant of the local Air Training Corps, a national cadet force, and Richard Jenkins, now Burton, was an NCO.

Selected cadets could be put forward as candidates for an elite route to aircrew-training. If chosen, they spent six months at Oxford or Cambridge University, a 'short course' that combined lectures with service training, before entering the RAF proper.

Richard Jenkins, miner's son, might have had difficulty getting past the selectors: Britain was in the middle of a desperate war, but class-consciousness flourished as usual. Richard Burton, schoolmaster's son, was a different matter.

In later life the actor dwelt proudly on the 'scholarship' he won to Oxford. In reality there was no scholarship. What mattered were the stripes on his uniform, his own character, and P.H. Burton's passionate advocacy.

Again there were touches of mysterious good fortune. Before young Burton went to Oxford, the Welsh writer and actor Emlyn Williams advertised in a Cardiff newspaper for a Welsh boy actor to appear in his new play, *The Druid's Rest*. 'P.H.' sent him off to audition in his uniform, and he was chosen, though for another part.

He appeared in provincial towns, ending up in a London theatre. The critic of the magazine *New Statesman* wrote that he showed 'exceptional ability.' Richard Burton said the two words changed his life.

At Oxford he wangled himself the part of Angelo, who is a sex-driven puritan, in an open-air production of Shakespeare's *Measure for Measure*. P.H. Burton came up from Wales to coach him. Robert Hardy, another actor-to-be who was there with Burton on the same course, was both riveted and chilled by the performance – 'a view into an unquiet soul,' he says now, in a phrase that could stand as an epitaph for Richard Burton's life.

In the audience one night was 'Binkie' Beaumont, the London impresario. The powerful Beaumont had an eye for talent and beauty, especially male beauty. He told Richard to come and see him after the war.

Above Emlyn Williams (left) gave Richard Burton, then aged 23, his first part in a film. Here, with actress Andrea Lea, they discuss Williams's script about an attempt to flood a Welsh valley for a reservoir. (H)

Below Emlyn Williams, Sybil Thorndyke and Richard Burton read Dylan Thomas's *Under Milk Wood* at the Old Vic in 1954. (H)

The war itself ended before he could go to Canada for aircrew training. As Aircraftman Second Class Burton, number 3025224, he spent two or three dull years, enlivened by occasional trips to London or Cardiff to appear in radio plays; once again 'P.H.', his guardian, was pulling strings.

Demobbed by the end of 1947, he went to see Beaumont, was signed up at £10 a week, and played small parts in the West End. But he was impatient, from the start. He told people that what he cared about was to escape the smell of poverty that lingered in his nostrils. Coalfield Wales, he would say, was vulgar but honest. The life was starved; he had no intention of settling there, although the place was agreeable enough to go back to.

Nearly forty years later, when he died after a lifetime of being written about as a man whose heart was always in his native land, he was buried in Switzerland. He had made his domicile there for tax reasons; and one useful way of proving 'domicile' in the legal sense is to buy a cemetery plot in the chosen land, and make arrangements to be buried there. In other words, Burton's estate would do better if he stayed away, even in death. It is all of a piece with the young actor's flight from the starved life of his youth, however fond he was of his family, a matter which no one disputes.

In 1947, the fact that London teemed with aspiring young actors coming out of the armed forces did not bother him unduly. The actor Richard Leech, beginning his career alongside Burton, was amazed to hear him say, 'Christ, if I can't make a living at this in another year, I'll give up.' Where was the dedication? What Burton seemed to have was a raw appetite for success, combined with an arrogant certainty of his ability to achieve it, whatever career he chose.

When Emlyn Williams offered him a good-sized part in a British film he was to write and direct, *The Last Days of Dolwyn*, Leech was even more amazed at the casual way Burton took the news. But Williams had recognized a face that the gods were going to be nice to – 'the startling looks, fearless green eyes set widely in a dramatic face: the face of a boxing poet.' Burton glided into the part, then into one or two bigger stage roles.

While working on *Dolwyn* he met Sybil Williams, a drama student who had talked her way into a small part. She was nineteen, an innocent beside Richard. She adored him. Years later, when Elizabeth Taylor was on the prowl, Burton assured a journalist, 'I'll never leave Sybil. She thinks I'm a genius.'

Soon there was talk of marriage. He sat up half the night in a flat in Hampstead, talking to a friend about her. She seemed to weigh on his mind, a responsibility, for once. Sitting motionless, staring into space, he said, 'Sybil is delightful and I love her dearly. And she assumes that having made love to her, I'll marry her. And so I suppose I shall.'

They were married in February 1949. 'It happened to be the day of a rugby

Burton's first real success on the stage
was in Christopher Fry's play, *The
Lady's Not for Burning*, in 1949. With him
is the young Claire Bloom, who was
later to play Ophelia to his Hamlet.
Their paths often crossed over the years.
(F) *Right* The play's author offers
Burton a sausage on a stick at a party to
celebrate the last night. Although the
play (in verse) had John Gielgud and
Pamela Brown as its stars, Burton, in a
small part, revealed a natural arrogance
that made people take notice. (H)

Prince of players: at the Stratford Memorial Theatre in 1951, the 26-year-old Burton becomes famous overnight, playing, first, Prince Hal, and then Henry V, in Shakespeare's historical cycle. 'A shrewd Welsh boy shines out with greatness,' wrote a critic. *Left* With Anthony Quayle (Falstaff), who chose him for the parts. As Henry V he was compared with Laurence Olivier, whose own King Henry was fresh in many people's memories. (H)

international,' says Philip Burton. 'Wales was playing Scotland. The bridegroom and his buddies decided to watch it on television. Worse than that, Wales lost. You never saw such a disgruntled wedding party in your life.'

Richard was still waiting for the 'big break', like a hundred others of his generation. A writer in the *New York Times*, reviewing a second British film in which he appeared, *Now Barabbas Was a Robber* (he played an Irish terrorist), compared him to the young Laurence Olivier. Olivier, already a leading figure in the British theatre before the war, had made a hit in Hollywood in 1938 with *Wuthering Heights*. Young Olivier wasn't a bad yardstick for young Burton to be measured against.

By Hollywood standards the modest black-and-white movies that he was appearing in were low-budget affairs. Still, they made him richer than most of his contemporaries.

As an Air Force officer in *The Woman With No Name*, a limping melodrama that nobody remembers now, he earned about a £1,000 for ten days' work. He bought a biggish house in north London, most of which he and Sybil rented out as apartments. The wolf was receding from the door.

And then, in 1951, came the chance he had been waiting for.

A couple of years earlier he had appeared in the West End in a fanciful verse comedy by Christopher Fry, *The Lady's Not For Burning*. The part was small, and he almost didn't get it because he was either nervous or drunk at the audition. But he acted alongside stars who included John Gielgud, and was noticed by one or two critics.

In 1950 he had a leading role in another Fry play, *The Boy With a Cart*, an uncommercial production outside the West End. Among those who saw it was the actor-director Anthony Quayle, who was to help mount the Shakespeare productions at Stratford-on-Avon the following year. Quayle was looking for a new young actor to play the Prince in *Henry IV*, and become the King in *Henry V*. He watched Richard Burton in a striped shirt with rolled-up sleeves, playing a shepherd with a divine mission, and looked no more.

The Stratford season of 1951 was part of the Festival of Britain, a kind of cultural and perhaps psychological rallying-point for the nation as the memory of war receded, and glimmerings of a 'New Elizabethan Age' were seen. It was not entirely an invention of publicists and headline writers. Change was in the air. The cycle of historical plays at Stratford reflected the mood of the time. An actor who could express it was sure of attention.

At Stratford that spring and summer, the weather was hot, the theatre crowded night after night. Richard Burton marched on to the stage in armour and leather, dark, boyish and brooding, and commanded attention.

Philip Burton, watching him and then reading what the newspapers said, could

Above The Last Days of Dolwyn (1948), Burton's first film. Burton and Dame Edith Evans, who played his foster mother, in a tense moment on the hillside, as villagers look on. Audiences liked the film, and its handsome young Welshman, though Burton later said his performance was 'lamentable'. (F)

Below The British film industry, still struggling to compete with Hollywood in the late 1940s, groomed Richard Burton as a 'leading man' before losing him to America. Here he is with Phyllis Calvert, in *The Woman with No Name* (1951), playing a young flying officer who has lost his memory. He earned £1,000: still a fortune, by his standards. (K)

hardly believe it was happening. He gave Richard 'notes' on his performances, but the strict pedagogue found little to correct. 'I feel ecstatically happy,' he wrote in his diary.

From the aloof Kenneth Tynan ('his playing turned interested speculation to awe') to the cheerful *Daily Mirror* ('Richard Shoots to Front as a Star'), critics sang his praises.

Long afterwards, Anthony Quayle, the man who found him for Stratford, looked back on that season, and remembered what a mixture of arrogance and talent Burton had been, cleverly using pauses and gestures to enhance his own performance at the expense of other actors around him on the stage.

No doubt the arrogance was part of the talent. What burst out at Stratford, said Quayle, was 'a latent power to disturb', some sexual quality that interested men and excited women.

In his first review, Tynan had quoted a 'dazed member' of the company as saying that Burton 'brings his cathedral on with him.' That made Quayle laugh. 'Actually,' he said, 'what Richard was thinking about was how soon he could get another pint of beer, or who he was going to sleep with next.'

Still, Burton's thoughts were his own. His performances in those regal parts were creations that separated themselves from him, like brilliant playing cards peeled off a pack, and began to make him famous.

The message reached the United States. He had already been there, the previous autumn, to play in *The Lady's Not For Burning* in New York. Now one or two notable Americans saw him at Stratford. Humphrey Bogart and Lauren Bacall, travelling in Europe, went there. So did talent scouts from Hollywood.

By summer the next year he would be in Los Angeles, shinning up an imitation house of wood and plaster, and kissing Olivia de Havilland on the balcony, as the cameras filmed *My Cousin Rachel*. When the film reached Port Talbot, people who had never been within fifty miles of Stratford and the Memorial Theatre would laugh out loud in the dark and say, 'Good grief, look at Richie Burton!'

In *Green Grow the Rushes* (1951) playing a smuggler. The girl with him is Honor Blackman, long before she starred in TV's *Avengers*. (S)

Right The film studios' image of Burton in 1951: dark and brooding. (K)

3

A STAR IN EXILE

THE TO-ING and fro-ing between London and Los Angeles, when Burton was pursuing two careers at once, lasted no more than four or five years. Oddly enough, he was not as successful in Hollywood as he had been at Stratford, and would be again during his two Old Vic seasons.

Equivalent acclaim in the world of cinema would have pushed him immediately into the superstar class. But in front of the cameras, his acting was inclined to be over-coloured and theatrical. Although women in the audience found him attractive enough, film somehow reduced his sexual appeal, instead of increasing it, as it might have done had he been a 'natural' film actor.

There is not necessarily anything 'better' about being a theatre actor. The point is that Burton, good as he was – sometimes – on film, ultimately lacked the impact in the big, populist world of the cinema that he once had in the small, elitist world of the London theatre.

It took years for this message to sink in, and in any case, film studios never treated him as anything less than important. But there was always a hint of some extra promise that ought to be fulfilled. Later in his career, of course, he became an international superstar, but that was after he met Elizabeth Taylor, sharing (and helping to enhance) the unique publicity she attracted. In his early Hollywood period, when he still regarded himself as a theatre actor, Burton was seen by film producers as a hot property of uncertain dimensions, to be handled with care.

He was on loan to Twentieth Century-Fox from the British film producer, Alexander Korda, whose company took a share of his American earnings. Twentieth Century wanted to sign him up for ten films, titles unknown. Burton discussed it, but refused.

They tried to put pressure on him. Invited to look in at the production office one morning, he found the room full of company executives who said it was too late for him to back out now. 'If you do,' said a lawyer, 'you'll never make another picture.'

Burton lost his temper. 'I haven't signed your effing contract,' he shouted, 'and as far as films are concerned, I prefer *acting*, on the stage. I did all right in London. As for suing me, I've got £30 in the post office.'

Burton took a cool view of the film business, which is to say that he poked fun at its self-importance, and gave the impression of keeping his distance, of being a visitor who didn't mean to stay. Thus he emphasized his Welshness, which

Burton's Hollywood début was in Daphne du Maurier's romantic story, *My Cousin Rachel* (1952), set in Cornwall but filmed in Los Angeles. His torrid screen relationship with his co-star, Olivia de Havilland, worried the censors, who made cuts in the script. (K)

intrigued the Hollywood columnists, and some of the hostesses as well. The idea that a bit of 'England' contained people like Burton, able to spout poetry and sing comic songs in a strange nasal language, was a novelty while it lasted.

Anyone who did suggest that 'Wales' was part of 'England' was promptly put right by Burton. They were different countries, he would say, both of them part of 'Britain', and he would go on to recite 'To be or not to be' in Welsh to prove it.

An account he gave of Hollywood survives. He was describing it for an Englishman who didn't know much about the place. It was April 1953, just as work on *The Robe* was nearing completion. The picture was a religious epic, of the kind that Hollywood used to love; much pious publicity surrounded the filming. Based on a famous novel about early Christians, it was said by its producer to have triumphed in the face of doubters (they feared it would cost too much) because Twentieth Century-Fox was receiving divine guidance. It was also the first film to be made in CinemaScope, the new wide-screen process that was supposed to be the cinema's answer to television.

Burton was unimpressed by the razzmatazz. 'It'll be indifferent, like all epics,' he told his friend. 'There's so much reverence and sentimentality around the studio, it makes me mentally throw up. We get cardinals and bishops – I decline to kiss their rings, since as you know I'm a staunch presbyterian – and a steady flow of nuns. Would you believe I've been asked not to smoke when the press are taking pictures? The whole place is fantasia. I haven't signed the contract they wanted me to, but I did agree to make another two or three films over the next few years. Now they're offering me £50,000 a picture, convinced that when I say No, it's because I'm trying to push the price up.'

There were four days' filming left on *The Robe*. After that, he and Sybil would have to stay for another month in case of retakes. They were going to move a few miles to Santa Monica and live in a bungalow by the sea. 'Strange,' he said, 'I thought films would be a holiday after the stage, but I'm on edge all the time. I have screaming fits on the set. I really think I hate this place. I despise most of the people in it, as well. They're all so bloody *frightened*. At the same time they lay on the flattery. It's obscene. *You're great!* they say. *Great! Great!* It's as if they'd invented a new cocktail, a Marlon-Brando-and-Burton, guaranteed to go to the head.'

His first season at the Old Vic was looming up. He was to play Hamlet, first at the Edinburgh Festival, then in London. 'One minute I'm belligerent about it, the next I'm apprehensive,' he said. 'I wake up sweating in the night. Then I go for a walk till I feel better. Oh for a real pint in a pub! Oh for a lot of things.'

Back in London, rehearsing his Hamlet, he continued to take night walks to calm his nerves. Philip Burton, who had given up schoolteaching to work for the BBC in London, helped to coach him. The director let him get on with interpreting

Above and right Hollywood saw *The Robe* (1953), the first film made in Cinemascope, as the cinema's answer to television. Burton had a powerful role as Marcellus, the Roman officer who is converted to Christianity. Jean Simmons, in love with Burton in the film, was another British player. The air of religiosity that surrounded the production didn't appeal to Burton. (K) (F)

the part in his own way: more than most of Shakespeare's characters, Hamlet is a vehicle for whatever an actor has to offer of himself.

The play opened in London to good but not ecstatic notices. Some critics found him too baleful, too forceful. Others compared him – again – to the Olivier of fifteen years earlier.

Winston Churchill went to see him perform, and met Burton in his dressing room. 'You were very virile, my Lord Hamlet,' he said.

The Robe was playing in cinemas at the same time. It received much publicity, and so did Burton. But it was no more than high-grade Hollywood junk. Burton's voice came over well, but his eyes looked dead.

Besides his Hamlet, Burton appeared in other plays during the Old Vic season, and got warmer notices – notably as the Bastard in *King John*, and in the name part in *Coriolanus*. There, as the tyrant, aloof from the mob, he came, said one reviewer, 'a sturdy stride nearer the greatness that so surely lies ahead of him.'

Thirty years later, when he had achieved almost everything he could once have hoped for, except for that elusive 'greatness', a sick and prematurely aged Burton would look back on the Old Vic season and say, '*Coriolanus* was written, as 'twere, for me. His arrogance and ruling of the mob is peculiarly myself.'

He spoke bitterly – it was in a BBC television interview – about his dislike of theatre-goers, an odd insight into a man who once seemed to base his life and hopes on the stage. 'Have you ever *looked* at an audience in the theatre?' he said. 'They are among the most vulgar people you've ever seen in your life.'

Was the scorn really for himself, for the way he had spent his life in a profession he never took seriously?

As a young man he was delighted to find he had a talent that could make him famous and wealthy, but he was disturbed by it as well. When he was rehearsing at Stratford, he told a radio producer that, 'Before I play Shakespeare I go through the text with Phil Burton. I'm just a marionette.' To Anthony Quayle he said he was frightened to find he had a 'gift', out of nowhere. 'I don't know what it is,' he said. 'If I ever started to know, I might lose it.'

As time went by, he would drift away from the uncertainty, the discipline and the drudgery of playing for the highest stakes. He found there were other flowers waiting to be picked.

There was one more bout of transatlantic commuting to come. Following the first Old Vic season of 1953–4, he was back in Hollywood for *The Rains of Ranchipur*, *The Prince of Players* (about an American Shakespearian actor; it flopped) and *Alexander the Great*, a turgid epic. Then London again for *Henry V* and *Othello*. Then Jamaica in the summer of 1956 to make a film with a sultry young star, Joan Collins, about a nun shipwrecked at sea, *Sea Wife*.

And that, as it turned out, was that. Richard Burton had flown the London

Having fought off the temptations of Hollywood film producers, who wanted him to stay there for good, Burton returned to Britain in 1953 to play a well-received Hamlet. 'You were very virile, my Lord Hamlet', Winston Churchill told him. Interest was heightened by the fact that Burton could also be seen in cinemas, starring in the Biblical spectacular *The Robe*. (S)

stage. By early 1957 he had bought a house in Switzerland, near Lake Geneva, and moved his legal residence out of Britain. From now on there would be tax problems if he came back to Britain for any length of time. It was both a reason and an excuse for giving up the hard grind of classical acting.

Becoming a tax exile is not an uncommon thing to do, but Burton received bad publicity for the move, as if he had somehow betrayed a trust that people had put in him. All he had done was decide that having paid many tens of thousands of pounds to the Inland Revenue, he wanted to pay no more. But, having been marked down as a future leader of the profession, there was a sense of irritation that he had said 'No, thanks', and pushed off to a foreign land.

In later life he would have loved a knighthood. He was famous enough for one, but not in the right way. He had to be content with C.B.E. after his name, Commander of the British Empire – respectable, but a long way from what he wanted.

One or two reporters went to see him and asked hypocritical questions about his being a tax dodger. Somebody sent him a letter addressed to 'Richard Burton, Welsh Actor, Tax-free Switzerland.' He thought it a good joke.

P.H. Burton, who seemed to fret more about Richard's career than Richard did himself, went to stay with him and Sybil on the French Riviera. 'Richard soon convinced me of the rightness of the big move,' he wrote in his diary. 'His happiness is good to see.'

The actor had just taken delivery of a Cadillac. Sybil was expecting a child. Aged thirty-one, Burton's life was taking a new direction. When his father died of a stroke in Wales, he didn't even go back for the funeral.

Still, he remained very much the Welshman. A BBC producer from Wales, who went to see him in Switzerland, was asked to bring film cans filled with laver bread, a Welsh seaweed eaten as a fried delicacy in Burton's part of the country. An elder brother, Ivor, of whom he was very fond, moved to Switzerland with him as a personal manager. Members of the family often went out to visit him, all expenses paid. And regular cheques were sent to brothers and sisters.

The new Burton didn't believe in working too hard. He made a mediocre war film, shot mainly in North Africa, called *Bitter Victory*, early in 1957. It was then a year and a half before he did another picture. He appeared in a stage play in New York, Jean Anouilh's *Time Remembered*, and in one or two television plays.

He also continued to make love to as many women as time and his life with Sybil allowed. Joan Collins, when she worked with him on *Sea Wife*, was propositioned while they were sunbathing on an offshore diving raft. Sybil was back at the hotel. Miss Collins tried to dissuade him by talking about her rich boy friend, but he continued to stroke her hair and fiddle with the top of her bikini. He gave up in the end, adding, however, that women always succumbed to him eventually.

During the rest of the filming, Miss Collins (who was soon engaged in a steamy

Above The Prince of Players gave Burton an excuse to play Shakespeare on the screen, in his role as the 19th century American actor, Edwin Booth, who took his company to mining camps in the West. (K)

Below In *Alexander the Great* (1956), still being shown on television, Burton gave a wooden performance in another of the 'giant, colossal, star-studded epics' that Hollywood used to make at regular intervals. (K)

Above Burton had too much style as a rule to let himself be used for studio 'beefcake' pictures. But they slipped in this one of him 'enjoying the tropical heat on the beach outside his hotel' in Jamaica, while filming *Sea Wife* in 1956. (K)

Opposite All adrift with Joan Collins, playing a nun in a dinghy in the 1957 movie *Sea Wife*. Miss Collins, star of *Dynasty* in the 1980s, had an off-screen encounter with Burton on a diving raft when they were on location. He told her that all women succumbed to him in the end, but she declined to be among them. (K)

affair with a young member of the camera crew) was amused to watch Burton consoling himself with other women. Some of them were attractive, some weren't.

In New York for the Anouilh play, he had a prolonged affair with an actress who appeared with him, Susan Strasberg; she was nineteen. It began before his wife and their small daughter Kate arrived from Switzerland, but continued unabated. They rented an apartment. He called her 'my pocket princess' and taught her to say she loved him very much, in Welsh.

She was even introduced to some of Burton's relatives when they came visiting. If these staunch chapelgoers ever realized that he not only had a mistress but was teaching her Welsh, the language of Heaven, they must have been shocked. In any case, there was nothing they could do about it. Ivor is said to have been the only brother who would tell Richard to his face to behave himself, and he doesn't appear to have achieved much.

An English actor, who was in the play, used to drink with Burton and hear about his sexual conquests. He formed the impression that it wasn't only lust that drove Burton – though it was that as well – but an exaggerated version of the actor's need to be loved. There was a certainty about women's bodies that Burton needed.

Time after time Burton would wave his hand and say, 'But it's all right, you see, I'd never leave Syb. I'd never let her know that I'm doing all this. I always say to the ladies, "I won't leave her, so I'm warning you now".'

The same actor noted that however much he drank, Burton never seemed to have much of a hangover. Nor did he ever give signs of being incapably drunk. He had a powerful constitution that thrived on alcohol but was able to contain it.

The decade had begun with great promise for Burton. It looked like ending with the promise unfulfilled. A screen version of John Osborne's stage play, *Look Back in Anger*, was made in Britain in 1959, with Burton playing the disillusioned Jimmy Porter. Claire Bloom was his co-star. It was his best film part so far, but his acting was too theatrical, even Shakespearian, and at thirty-three he was too old for the part.

The following year he made two undistinguished pictures for Warner Brothers in Hollywood, *The Bramble Bush* and *Ice Palace*. The latter was an Alaskan saga, with a script so poor that the man they asked to direct it, Vincent Sherman, agreed only because he thought privately that the studio would be unable to cast it.

In the event he was wrong. Warner found enough people who wanted the money. Burton, playing a hard-faced tycoon, was hired for $125,000. Sherman became friendly with him as the film progressed, and liked him immensely. 'Why in hell did you agree to it?' he asked. 'Very simple,' said Burton. 'They're paying me for eight weeks' work, and I realized that no director could possibly make this movie in eight weeks. It'll take you a lot longer. Then they'll have to pay me

In *Bitter Victory* (1957) Burton played a commando in the desert, disenchanted with war. It was one of the first films he made after he moved to Switzerland for tax reasons. His role was unconvincing; so was the picture. (K)

Above After six years of marriage, Richard and Sybil Burton seemed as happy as ever. She was a realist and put up with her husband's infidelities. Here – in the summer of 1955 – they catch a boat train from London *en route* to Hollywood for another bout of film-making. (F)

Opposite Soon after he escaped British taxes and went to live in Switzerland, Richard Burton was a millionaire. His house at Celigny, near Geneva, was called 'Pays de Galles', the French for 'Wales'. With his wife Sybil and their first child, Kate, he made a retreat from the world of film-sets and airliners. But his happy life with Sybil was coming to an end. (R)

Although he was really too old (at 33) to play the rebellious Jimmy Porter in the screen version of John Osborne's *Look Back in Anger* (1959), the role was an improvement on some of the parts that Hollywood had been asking him to play. *Above* With Gary Raymond and Claire Bloom. *Below* With Raymond again, and the director, Tony Richardson. (K)

overage' (the cinema actor's equivalent of overtime). Burton was quite right. He earned a quarter of a million dollars, double the original fee.

'If you're going to make rubbish,' Burton told reporters, 'be the best rubbish in it,' adding impertinently, 'I keep telling Larry Olivier that.'

Having said one thing, he then did the opposite. He stopped making rubbish, whether by accident or design, and spent 1960 on projects he had no need to apologize for. One was a short play written for British television by John Osborne, *A Subject of Scandal and Concern*. The director who cast him for the part was Tony Richardson, who had made *Look Back in Anger*. The BBC paid Burton £1,000, grumbling that they had never paid an actor on that scale, although it was pocket money beside his cinema earnings.

The play was based on the true story of a nineteenth-century schoolmaster who ruined himself by standing up for his radical principles. Burton turned himself into a stammering little man wearing spectacles to give an admirable 'character' performance, of a kind he rarely if ever attempted again.

In the United States he narrated twenty-six episodes of a television documentary called *The Valiant Years*, based on Churchill's war memoirs, earning lots of dollars and much praise.

But the key event of 1960, in retrospect the hinge on which his career turned, was his appearance on Broadway in the stage musical *Camelot*. This elegant spectacular (known in the trade as 'Costalot') about King Arthur and the Knights of the Round Table gave him a kingly part in a popular production, where he could use the full range of his voice, for singing as well as speaking.

Together with the Churchill series, it made him a new reputation in America. That was how he came to be considered for a leading part in a production that was to become one of the great movie circuses, a monument to absurdity. He was offered a part in *Cleopatra*.

4
RICHARD AND ELIZABETH

E VEN WITHOUT the affair between Richard Burton and Elizabeth Taylor, the making of *Cleopatra* would have been an extravagant affair. Originally planned in 1958, it was first seen by Twentieth Century-Fox as a pot-boiler, a 'tits and sand' picture costing less than a million dollars, starring any capable actress with a good bosom.

Over the next couple of years the plan was upgraded. Brigitte Bardot and Marilyn Monroe were both contemplated as Cleopatras. By 1960 it was to be Taylor. The film company was in financial difficulties, and a big picture with her was seen as the way to salvation. Mark Antony at this point was going to be Stephen Boyd.

While Taylor and her lawyers were demanding a guaranteed fee of a million dollars, the studio got ready to begin shooting in a fake Alexandria that had been built at Pinewood studios, outside London. Since the English weather was not much like Egypt's, hundreds of extras would turn up at huge cost, only to be sent home again because of fog.

Then Taylor became ill, even before she started work. She had an infected tooth. While she recovered, the studio abandoned little-Egypt-in-England and brought in a new director, Joseph Mankiewicz.

Mankiewicz, something of an intellectual, had seen Burton in *Camelot*, and wanted to hire him. At first the studio wasn't keen, remembering how he hadn't quite shone as expected, seven or eight years earlier, in pictures like *The Robe*. Eventually the director got his way.

In the spring of 1961, Taylor was ill again, and in the London Clinic. This time she nearly died; there could scarcely have been more publicity if she had. Her husband at the time was Eddie Fisher, not long divorced amid noisy scandal from the actress Debbie Reynolds. She had also been having an affair with a middle-aged professor.

Everything about her – sex, health, temper, acting, jewels, hairstyles, waistline – was news. Twentieth Century, more desperate than ever to have her for the film, gave her what she asked for, and photography for *Cleopatra* began in Rome in September.

Burton, having been bought out of *Camelot*, is supposed to have said before he left for Italy that he had to 'don my breastplate once more to play opposite Miss Tits.' He was being paid a quarter of a million dollars for three months' work, but

40

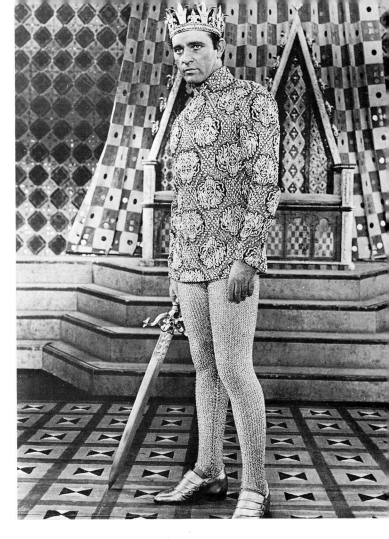

Above A small-town story about scandal and euthanasia, *The Bramble Bush* (1960) was one of several pictures that Burton starred in, after Hollywood had lost its first enthusiasm for him, and before *Cleopatra* gave him a second start. (K)

Right above Burton took to his role of King Arthur, in the New York production of the smash-hit musical *Camelot* in 1960, like a duck to water. The fantasy-king was a role that appealed to one side of his nature. As a result of *Camelot* he got the part of Mark Antony in *Cleopatra*. (K)

Right below Journalists said it was the biggest story to come out of Rome, barring the death of Popes. Even allowing for exaggeration, the sexual goings-on between Richard Burton and Elizabeth Taylor were front-page news. (R) at first had little to do. He was in few scenes at the beginning, and none involving Taylor.

With him in Rome was his wife and their two children, Kate, now four years old, and Jessica, aged two – although the second daughter had been mentally retarded from birth, and little was ever said about her, then or later. Ivor was in attendance, Burton's assistant and his conscience.

There is a persistent story that Burton and Taylor started their affair before they came together in Rome. One or two of his close relatives say he told them it began in New York, when he was still appearing in *Camelot*.

Whether or not this is true, the Fishers and the Burtons met socially in Rome, and there was ample opportunity for the Welshman to impress the superstar, and vice-versa. By the end of the year, some of the production team knew, or thought they knew, that the two were sleeping together.

It took another few weeks for the news to leak out. They played their first scene together on 22 January 1962. He was dressed in a toga, she in yellow silk. Burton had a hangover, with a blotchy face and trembling hands. Those who didn't know already thought they could detect that 'something' was going on.

Eddie Fisher heard the rumours within a week or so. When journalists heard them, and rang the studio, they were told it was all lies. The more it was denied, the more the rumours circulated. Was it true they disappeared into her dressing room for hours on end? Was it true they had been seen embracing in the back of a car?

Twentieth Century wanted all the publicity it could get from Elizabeth Taylor's behaviour, but not if it meant her cavorting with a married actor, a year or two after she had done the same sort of thing with Eddie Fisher. Public morals were stricter in 1962.

Burton himself was told by his brother Ivor to behave himself. This was not an affair that the press would shrug its shoulders over. Burton had been seeing at least one other lover in Rome, an American girl, but that was unexceptional. The affair with Taylor, once it became public gossip, would be difficult for Sybil to ignore, as she had ignored other episodes. The two brothers went to Naples together to talk. Ivor was insistent: he didn't like the woman, and Richard had to put an end to the affair. But it was easier said than done.

The film's producer, Walter Wanger, asked Burton in for a talk.

'Am I fired?' said Burton.

Wanger said No, why should he be?

'Because of the rumours. They're as embarrassing to me as they are to you. I'm a selfish man and I don't want anything to interfere with my career. I'm happy with Sybil. And I won't do anything to harm Liz.'

None of the fine talk had any effect. Italian newspapers buzzed with the affair.

Sybil flew to New York to see Philip Burton, who now lived there – ostensibly because he was ill, in fact because she was relying on him to influence her husband. 'P.H.' hesitated, then sent a telegram reproving Richard, asking him what on earth he was thinking about. It was an unwise message to send in uncoded language in a city with as many journalists as Rome, and the press got hold of it. The actor was furious. He telephoned his mentor, called him indiscreet and naive, and banged the phone down. It was another two years before they spoke.

For a long time everyone in Burton's circle believed that sooner or later he would 'come to his senses,' drop Elizabeth Taylor and be reconciled with Sybil. Twenty years later Cecilia, the sister who brought him up, could still say that 'we all rue the day he met Elizabeth.'

Perhaps Burton himself thought it would end in reconciliation. He said it was 'a kind of nightmare' – making the film, dodging the pursuing journalists, consorting with his lover, talking endlessly on the phone to his wife, who by now was back in Switzerland. He was sure the telephone was tapped. He told friends that he carried a knife, though it wasn't clear what for.

On the set he worked with his usual vigour and competence, but there were flashes of savage temper. When Mankiewicz, the director, himself harassed beyond belief by the production, had to shoot a horseback scene several times, Burton screamed, 'Can't you bastards get the thing right once? Don't you know what bloody torture it is, riding through this crowd?'

With *Cleopatra* finished by the summer of 1962, Taylor and Burton went away together for a few weeks, then seemed to separate. But the affair was not suspended for long. They were both in Switzerland. Burton was with Sybil and the children at their house in Celigny, near Geneva. Taylor, her marriage to Eddie Fisher effectively at an end, was at Gstaad, seventy miles away. More than once that autumn, Burton drove to meet her, then back to Celigny in the small hours of the morning; he boasted to relatives how his car came screaming up the empty roads.

His marriage crumbled slowly, doing maximum damage to all concerned. Burton was said to be 'maddened with guilt.' Guilt or no, it was soon announced that before the end of the year, he and Taylor were to star in a new film to be made in London, *The VIPs*. By December they were all there. Sybil was in a house they owned in Hampstead that the press didn't know about. Burton and Taylor were both at the Dorchester Hotel, occupying separate suites to keep up appearances.

The film, written by Terence Ratigan for MGM, had been in the air long before the Burton–Taylor liaison. Now that they were the world's best-known adulterers – with no sign that shocked audiences were going to start boycotting Twentieth Century productions – MGM decided to join the bandwagon.

Burton's agents were able to get him the best contract of his life, so far, with guaranteed earnings of half a million dollars for ten weeks' work. A thousand dollars a week 'expenses' were thrown in. Taylor was guaranteed a million. But he couldn't complain; his own value had doubled since *Cleopatra*, before the Roman blockbuster had even been released. Studio memos two years later show that eventually he earned another half a million for his percentage of *VIP* box-office takings.

At last he had arrived in the big-earnings league. No one can say whether, under other circumstances, he might have arrived there under his own steam. He must have wondered about it himself. Looked at in one way, it was an accident that he made *Cleopatra* and fell in love with its leading lady. But Burton was probably enough of a realist to accept that people have a knack of putting themselves in the way of accidents like that.

His friends speculated (and still do, over long drinks and longer memories) about how Elizabeth succeeded in taking him from Sybil and changing his life. Was she clever or just lucky? Was Burton somehow bewitched by her sexuality, unable to break the spell until it was too late? Or, which seems more likely, was he just an insatiable man, doing what his bones told him to?

'I don't want anything to interfere with my career,' he told Walter Wanger. He didn't say what kind of career he had in mind, but there can be little doubt that he wanted fame and riches in the cinema, and all the trappings that went with stardom at the highest level. He wanted journalists to sit and listen while he talked about poetry and women and the agonies of Celtic melancholy. He wanted the obedient circle of network cameras, bowing their lenses. He wanted to rise up in the public imagination, and in the end he did.

Meanwhile, six months after *Cleopatra*, his private life was tormented. People noticed that Taylor clung to him more closely than he to her. He still had a wife who wanted him back, and from time to time he would slip away to see her. When he was seen walking with her in Hyde Park, there was panic among MGM officials in London in case Taylor found out.

Of his wife's grief there were few public traces. She was reticent, wounded, by nature not a thrower of scenes. In a few years she was to make a career of her own in New York as impresario and night-club owner. She married a man twelve years her junior, and, at thirty-six, had a child by him. But as long as Burton hesitated between the two women, she lived in hope.

'She used to come down and drink endless crèmes de menthe with us,' says an actor, a close friend of Burton and his wife. 'We drove her back to Hampstead late one night, and unfortunately I took the shortest way from Chelsea, which was straight up Park Lane, where the Dorchester is. By this time Sybil and my wife were both in tears, and suddenly Sybil said, "There are the lights, that's the suite he's in, that's where he is with the bitch". And I said, being deeply in drink, "Right, I'll get him out".

'I drove up to the front of the Dorchester – daylight was just beginning – and I went up to the hall porter, taking our dog, which we'd brought with us. I said I was so-and-so, just back from New York, and if you give Mr Burton my name, I think he'll come down. They kept saying he wasn't to be disturbed. I argued and argued, and then I looked around and saw that the dog had peed on the carpet, which absolutely defeated me. I said I'd call him at lunchtime, and left.'

The same friends found themselves entertaining Richard and Elizabeth at their house. When the two left, Taylor seized her host's arm and whispered, 'Don't hate me', which sounds like a line from a script, but was only in keeping with the theatrical overtones of the affair. There were continual fears of suicide attempts. Sybil was seen to have scars on her wrists.

Gradually things sorted themselves out. Sybil moved to New York. A divorce settlement of a million and a half dollars was reported. Money poured out. It also poured in. 'Richard and Elizabeth' became an established combination. *Cleopatra* was released, to groans from the critics and packed cinemas. Much the same happened with *The VIPs*. The Burtons were the stuff that studio dreams are made of.

5

DIVORCE HIS...DIVORCE HERS

THE FIRST artistic fruits of Burton's relationship with Elizabeth Taylor were promising. He became wealthier than ever, but not by appearing in rubbish, even the best kind. He admitted in public that Elizabeth Taylor had taught him a lot about film acting, including the fact that 'my very penetrating voice needn't be pitched louder than a telephone conversation.' Most of all, he said, she taught him to take film acting seriously.

In *Becket*, a film about royal England in the twelfth century, he gave a striking performance in the name part, the Archbishop. In *The Night of the Iguana*, filmed in Mexico late in 1963, John Huston directed him as a broken-down priest who is working as a tour guide, and ends up with his party in a rotting hotel at the back of beyond. Taylor and her staff of maids and assistants were at the insect-ridden location throughout, although she wasn't in the film.

The pair were still unmarried, but already they had settled into their public routine of affection laced with tears and a trace of violence. Every time Burton's hairdresser attended to his hair, Elizabeth would add a few loving touches of her own. Exasperated by this, he grabbed a bottle of beer and poured it over his head.

'Look at her,' he said affectionately. 'She walks just like a French tart.' In the evenings, full of drink, he would recite poetry to anyone in earshot. 'The only thing in life is language,' he boomed. 'Not love, not anything else.' This upset Taylor, who started weeping. In the past, Burton could have done all manner of things on a film location, and probably did, without having it noted. Now his new fame, and the presence of Elizabeth Taylor, meant that reporters were often around and film employees kept diaries.

His Hamlet on Broadway the following year brought enormous crowds. Critics praised his 'virility' and 'electricity.' He was a man of the cinema, taking films as they came; for the rest of his life, the theatre would be incidental.

Any notion that he had turned his back on rubbish for good was dispelled by the first picture that he and Elizabeth Taylor made together as husband and wife, *The Sandpiper* in 1965. He was a clergyman again, this time with a wife, who sins with a poor young woman living on the beach – at least, that was the original idea, until the woman became Elizabeth Taylor, looking well-fed and elegant, with twenty-two costume changes. They sinned improbably in a lavish beach house (specially constructed in Paris, where they insisted on filming for tax reasons). The film, needless to say, made money.

On the set of one of Burton's best films, *The Night of the Iguana*, where he played an alcoholic priest. Here seen on the set with three of his co-stars (from left), Sue Lyons, Deborah Kerr and Ava Gardner. Elizabeth Taylor kept a close eye on him during filming. (K)

On the other hand, Burton (not Taylor) in *The Spy Who Came In from the Cold*, based on John Le Carré's novel, was a very satisfactory, solid-shabby double agent. And in 1965 they came together in their happiest coupling of talents to film the screaming, shouting domestic claw fight of Edward Albee's *Who's Afraid of Virginia Woolf?*

As George and Martha, trapped in their fearful marriage, they gave convincing performances that contained unintentional hints of their own raw-edged behaviour towards one another in their private lives.

'I can't stand it!' George shouts at Martha.

'You can stand it,' she shouts back. 'You married me for it.'

Burton had his fortieth birthday while making the picture. One moment he was heard to say that he suffered from bouts of homesickness for Britain, that he wanted to go back for good and 'pay taxes like everyone else.' The next, that he would wake in the middle of the night, aching for a walk in London, but 'wouldn't much like the thought of paying those exorbitant taxes.' You paid your money and you took your choice. The homesick Welshman was a fantasy figure with which to amuse himself.

The real Burton had houses in Mexico and Switzerland and Los Angeles. His income was channelled through Atlantic Programmes, registered in Bermuda, and other companies designed to minimize tax. Much of his wealth was tied up in property holdings and family trusts. He employed lawyers and accountants, though not on the same scale as his wife, and the two of them travelled with cooks, hairdressers, secretaries and bodyguards.

He liked to have the best seat in a plane, the best table in a restaurant. It was natural that he should, given his circumstances. But he always tried to have jam on it, to conjure up some other Burton, who was a working-class boy with uncon-summated longings, who had dark dreams and wanted to write books, and wasn't taken in by the cheap glitter of success. One side of him scorned the glitter; the other went ahead and enjoyed it. It was as though he was the grit in his own oyster.

In front of other people, Richard and Elizabeth gave unscripted performances from an endless soap opera about two stars locked in a turbulent, ecstatic relationship.

Lunch is served in their suite in a New York hotel. Kate, his daughter by Sybil, ten years old, is with them. Elizabeth looks at the wine.

'I thought you ordered Laffitte-Rothschild, Richard. What's this junk? Are you trying to save money again?'

Presently he turns to her and snaps, 'What does *viable* mean? Quickly. *Supine*. *Docile*. What do they mean?'

'Do you ever give yourself the creeps, love?' she says.

48

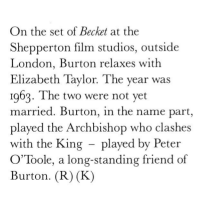

On the set of *Becket* at the
Shepperton film studios, outside
London, Burton relaxes with
Elizabeth Taylor. The year was
1963. The two were not yet
married. Burton, in the name part,
played the Archbishop who clashes
with the King – played by Peter
O'Toole, a long-standing friend of
Burton. (R) (K)

'Come on.'

She licks ice cream from a spoon. 'I think you are prolix and verbose.'

When she goes to her bedroom to dress, she is heard calling, 'What shall I wear, Richard, to go look at the jewellery?'

'Why don't you go naked?' he shouts.

Elizabeth reappears. 'That's Dada, babes, that's him. Just watch your language avec moi, Richard, just watch it.'

Every year he made two or three pictures, clocking up, among others, a colourful Shakespeare with Taylor (*The Taming of the Shrew*), a gloomy Graham Greene adaptation (*The Comedians*), a showy Marlowe for charity (*Dr Faustus*), an absurd Tennessee Williams fantasy, also with Taylor (*Boom!*), a bird-brained sexual romp with Marlon Brando in it (*Candy*) and a decent World War II thriller (*Where Eagles Dare*).

By now he was able to get a guaranteed million dollars for a picture. His contract for *Where Eagles Dare*, drawn up between MGM and Atlantic Programmes in 1967, shows how far he had travelled in ten years.

His million dollars were to cover sixteen weeks' work, and they were paid to Atlantic in sixteen weekly instalments of $62,500. On top of this were 'living expenses' of $50,000. First-class travel for Burton and up to seven others, from anywhere in the world to the first filming location, and from the last location to anywhere else in the world, was included. Wherever Burton went, a 'deluxe chauffeured limousine' was to be available, twenty-four hours a day.

These are the raw materials of opulence. In addition, Burton's approval was needed of the director. Burton's name must go in first position, in letters at least as large as the title. And he didn't have to work on 1 March, the day of St David, patron saint of Wales – a condition he came to insist on in all his contracts.

Years later, Burton said that he and Elizabeth were happy for the first seven years. That time was up in 1968, the year in which he made *Where Eagles Dare*, and also the year when his drinking became noticeably heavier. Whether this caused problems with his wife, or whether the problems were the reason for the drinking, is anyone's guess.

He had always been a serious drinker, like the other Welshman whose poetry he doted on from adolescence, Dylan Thomas. When he was making the *Spy* movie, he was heard to say he had broken 'all my own admirable records' because of a shot that called for him to drink a large whisky.

'It was the last shot of the day,' he said, 'and I decided to use the real hard stuff. We did forty-seven takes. Imagine it, love, forty-seven whiskies.' He was echoing Thomas's alleged remark in New York about the drinking bout that killed him, 'Eighteen straight whiskies. I think that's the record.' But, being Richard Burton, he had to make it a bit more.

Right A shabbier Burton came to the surface in *The Spy Who Came In from the Cold*, the film of John Le Carré's novel. Burton gave an outstanding performance as the British double-agent. (K)

Below 'I can't stand it!' George screamed at Martha. 'You can stand it,' she screamed back. 'You married me for it'. Burton and Taylor (here with George Segal) re-created an unhappy marriage in *Who's Afraid of Virginia Woolf* (1966). Their own life together had more than a touch of the George and Marthas. (K)

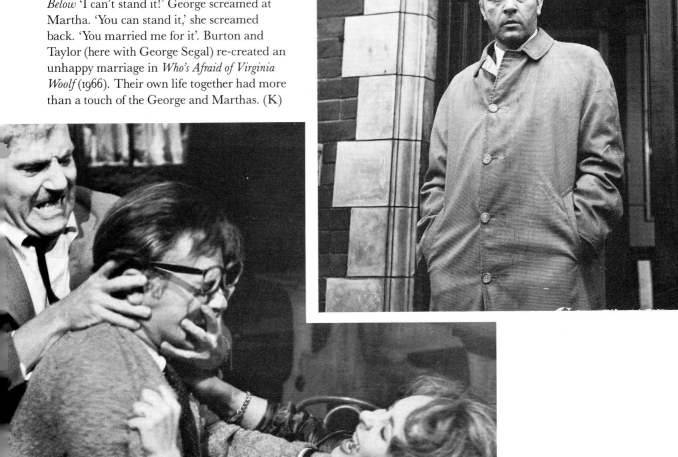

He said he drank because 'Celts have this black cell that makes them go off and drink.' Or it was because he was an actor – 'Acting is somehow shameful for a man to do. It isn't natural to put on make-up and wear costumes on stage and say someone else's lines. So you drink to overcome the shame.' Or it was because he was bored. Or (in his Shakespearian mood) it was 'because the world is so infinitely full of pain and riches, and occasionally you have to kill the pain by drinking.' In the silence, the only sound was the scribbling of pencils.

By 1968 and perhaps earlier, he was an alcoholic – not the first actor to need the bottle, but the most forthcoming on the subject. 'From 1968 to 1972,' he once said, 'I was pretty hopeless. I was fairly sloshed for five years. I was up there with Jack Barrymore and Robert Newton' – two other actors with thirsts. 'The ghosts of them were looking over my shoulder.'

It was a lot more than five years. Film producers began to worry that he might collapse on the set and cost them money; but however much vodka or whisky he had inside him, he soldiered on. When he was filming *Anne of the Thousand Days* in 1969 at the British Shepperton studios, they had difficulty getting him out of the local pub after lunch. He wasn't visibly drunk, but he was profoundly indifferent to the part.

One afternoon he was needed for a close-up scene where only his top half would be visible. 'I'll keep my own shoes and trousers on,' he said. The king in sports slacks was duly filmed. It was just one of Burton's jokes. A well-known Shakespearian actor who was on the set was disgusted. Perhaps that was why Burton did it.

Universal Pictures in Hollywood was on edge when it hired Burton for a month to shoot a quickie film in Mexico, *Raid on Rommel*, the following year. Stories of his self-destructive drinking were commonplace by now. 'We stayed in a motel on the edge of a little town,' says the producer. 'I was scared to death.'

The picture was designed to use up action footage of tank battles and men being killed, shot years earlier for a picture called *Tobruk*, and left over from the editing. The long shots were then intercut with new close-up material, using Burton and other actors, filmed in a roughly comparable bit of desert. Burton said he was so fascinated at such an impudent idea that he couldn't resist it.

The producer waited for the drinking to start. Nothing happened. Burton (who had Taylor with him) was sober and well-behaved. He didn't complain about the frontier conditions. He was never late on the set. (And the film wasn't bad, all things considered).

But although he had too much style to be predictable, there were persistent signs that Burton was descending a ladder. When he made a bad film now, it was likely to be in a new category of badness. This may have reflected an indifference on his part to what pictures he made, as well as a reluctance by film studios to engage him in productions where his drinking could seriously hurt them.

Burton's New York Hamlet, in 1964, packed the theatre for 134 performances. Directed (in rehearsal clothes) by John Gielgud, it was one of Burton's rare appearances in a classic role after his last Old Vic season in 1956. *Above* On stage with Eileen Herlie (the Queen). *Right* With Elizabeth Taylor (who called him 'the Frank Sinatra of Shakespeare') and an American publisher. (R)

In *The Assassination of Trotsky*, despite the attentions of a distinguished director, Joseph Losey, his performance as the Russian exile was as halting as the rest of the picture. In *Hammersmith Is Out*, he played an evil lunatic, but it was hard to tell what was supposed to be going on.

Bluebeard was a potboiler with pretty girls, made in Hungary in 1972, when Taylor's fortieth birthday was celebrated at a Budapest party that went on all weekend. Burton gave her a heart-shaped diamond, holding it up for photographers and saying, 'it has so many carats, it's almost a turnip.' In case anyone thought the Budapest caper was in bad taste, the Burtons said they would give an amount equivalent to its cost to the United Nations Children's Emergency Fund. A cheque for $45,000 was later handed over.

Actresses, gossip columnists, pop stars, minor royalty and Burton's family were among the guests in Budapest. All expenses paid, including caviare and bloaters, said the telegrams inviting people. A private suite was provided for his brothers to watch video tapes of the Welsh rugby team playing international matches; only matches that Wales had won were chosen. There was a spot of bother when the novelist Alan Williams, a son of the Emlyn Williams who had been one of Burton's early mentors, made some aggressive remarks to Taylor about there not being many Hungarians at the party. She burst into tears, and her minders came running and threw him out. His description of her, 'a beautiful doughnut covered in diamonds and paint' was gleefully repeated.

During the party Burton was observed to be drinking soda water. Optimists saw signs that he was going to pull himself together. A proposal that he spend a term or even a year at an Oxford college, teaching Shakespeare, had received much attention. He was said to be anxious to 'recharge his batteries.'

His brief stay at the university as an officer-cadet in 1944 had become a small golden age for him to recall. The talk about going there in the 1970s might be a good sign if he was serious, but a bad sign if Oxford was merely another of his fantasies. A Fellow of St Peter's College, Francis Warner, a friend of the Burtons, arrived at the Budapest party with the offer of an honorary fellowship. Burton said, 'Thank you very much.' But nothing came of the plan, if it was a plan.

Another story circulated, that Burton had been asked to take over as director of the National Theatre when Laurence Olivier retired. Burton gave his friends detailed accounts. 'I'm getting disenchanted with acting,' he said. 'It's ludicrous to have to keep learning the lines of some idiot just to stay a millionaire. Larry Olivier asked me to take over from him – in tandem to start with, then alone. When I said No, it shook him savagely. I've rarely felt so sorry for a man.'

If the offer was actually made to Burton, it must have been on an informal basis. Philip Burton says it was true that Olivier would have liked Richard, under the right circumstances. But that would have meant changing his way of life, not

Film studios were quick to cash in on the Burton-and-Taylor connection, casting them together in films with sexual undercurrents. In *The Sandpiper* he was a clergyman and she was an artist who lives by the Pacific. The nude statue of her was part of the general titillation. *Right* Having lunch on the set. (K)

simply making a few cosmetic adjustments. Burton told a friend that if he returned to London permanently, it would cost him two million pounds in back tax.

The month after the Budapest party, Richard's brother Ivor died. He was only sixty-six, but for four years had been paralysed following an accident. Burton hinted that grief started him drinking again. 'I kept having the same nightmare,' he said. 'I thought he was there in the room with me, smiling.'

The more he drank, the more he and Elizabeth Taylor quarrelled. In public they remained the fiery lovers that the world wanted to read about. But some of their admirers, at least, were getting tired of the diamonds, the yacht, the boasting, the posturing.

Their last film work together was, or became, yet another attempt to cash in on their fading glamour. Written as two linked screen plays, *Divorce His* and *Divorce Hers*, it was about a rich husband and wife whose marriage has broken up, meeting in Rome to rake over their past. The films were made for television, with some of the money put up by Harlech, the Welsh television station, in which the Burtons had an interest.

According to the director, Burton remained sober to start with. They were preparing to film a night scene in Rome when Elizabeth Taylor, who wasn't due there for another two days, arrived unexpectedly. A small crowd had been watching the film unit at work. Suddenly there were blaring horns, police, photographers running, and in the middle of it all a black limousine from which Elizabeth emerged. 'Don't worry about me,' she purred. 'I'll just stand in the corner and watch.' Burton had disappeared. By the time they found him he was drunk. All he had to do in the shot was walk down the street and turn, but it took nine or ten attempts to get it right.

Most of the filming was done in Munich. By the afternoons he was always the worse for drink. The director had lunch with the Burtons and their entourage one day, sitting next to Burton, whose acting in the London theatre he had admired. He told him so, and Burton, pleased at having his Hamlet and Coriolanus recalled, launched into one of his comic monologues, about playing the Prince in *Henry IV*, wearing chain mail and armour, after he had been drinking beer. He had to relieve himself inside the armour.

It was a good story, told often enough before, but new to the director. Before Burton got to the end, he caught his wife's eye and stopped.

'Come on, Richard,' she said.

'Elizabeth's bored by it,' he explained. 'She's heard it so many times.'

'Oh *no*, Richard,' she said. 'I'm always *fascinated* to know what a wonderful stage actor you were.'

He didn't finish the story.

Later in the lunch they talked about the German child that Elizabeth Taylor

Previous page and above and opposite Franco Zeffirelli's film production of *The Taming of the Shrew* (1967) brought the Burtons together for one of their happier film partnerships. It seemed to reflect something of the conflicts in their private lives, but in an amiable way. Burton called the film 'a great mudpie-in-the-face romp'. (K)

In 1966, the Burtons went to Oxford to take part in a university production of Marlowe's *Dr Faustus*. More than one critic saw Burton himself as a Faustus-figure, selling out to the Devil – or at least to Mammon. Elizabeth Taylor had a non-speaking part as Helen of Troy, conjured up by magic for his pleasure. Professor Nevill Coghill, with the Burtons (*opposite above*) produced the play. He had admired Richard since he gave him a wartime part in a Shakespeare play. (K) (F) (S)

Opposite below Burton would like, he said, to have been an academic and enjoyed returning to Oxford to give 'tutorials'. (H)

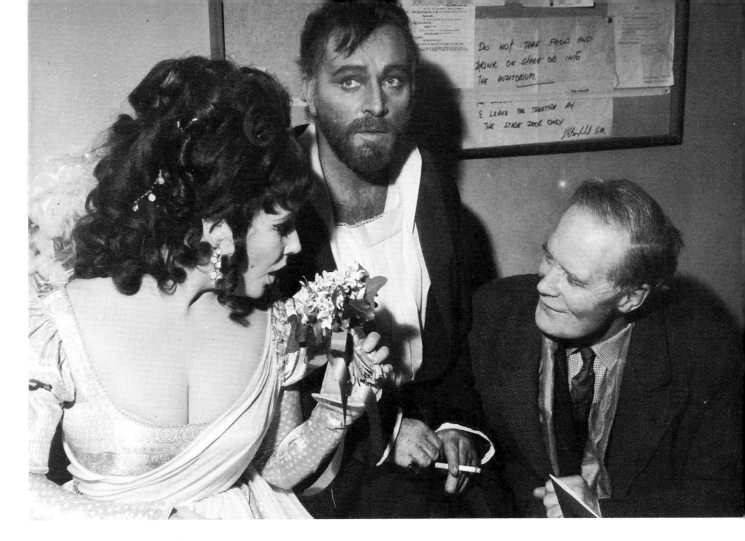

had adopted in 1962, when she was still married to Eddie Fisher, just as her affair with Burton was beginning. The child, Maria, had been sickly, with a crippled hip, but expensive treatment had cured her.

'We're very fond of our daughter,' said Burton at one point.

'*Your* daughter, Richard?' snapped his wife. 'You weren't even on the scene when I found her, for God's sake. Just because she has your name . . .'

No doubt both of them were unhappy. In Burton's case what made it worse was that at last he seems to have woken up and realized that he hated the kind of life he was leading. As he staggered from one bad picture to another – the *Divorce* films were the ultimate advertisement of his fallen state – he knew that all eyes were on his real-life marriage. He told a (platonic) woman friend, 'We were so under the magnifying glass, every time we moved, everything became exaggerated. What would normally be a little outburst of temper or recalcitrance or whatever, if we were two people who lived in a suburb, was blown up.'

In May the following year, 1973, he was in Italy with his wife, who was making a film called *Ash Wednesday*. Instead of her sitting idly while he filmed, it was the other way around. The location was a couple of hours from Venice by road, halfway up a mountain. There was nothing to do but ski, which didn't interest Burton. People saw him sitting alone in the lobby of the hotel, reading the English papers, a bottle by his side.

'I was drinking pretty hard at that time,' Burton told the platonic friend. 'Elizabeth was doing a film I didn't approve of. I told her so. "Very good script and all that," I said, "but I don't like the thought of you in it because it represents the worst kind of people. The jet set and stuff like that – face-lifts and breast-lifts". I was terribly pompous. Anyway, she went ahead and made it, and I sat around, loathing every second, with nothing to do except read. I wouldn't have minded if she was doing Lady Macbeth or something. But my soul was affronted.

'I really don't like the jet set, you know. They offend me. They do funny things, smoke the wrong things, drugs and stuff like that, and I really can't bear them.'

Soon after that, in the summer of 1973, the Burtons separated. Journalists tracked him down to a friend's house on Long Island, drinking vodka and orange juice at ten in the morning, babbling whatever came into his head. Elizabeth Taylor, never failing to behave as Stars were expected to, put out a statement to say that 'maybe we have loved each other too much.' For a while she consoled herself with a new lover, while Burton went to stay in Rome with Sophia Loren and her film-producer husband, Carlo Ponti. But when Elizabeth was taken ill and went into hospital to see if she had cancer – she hadn't – he flew to California and they were reunited with the magic words, 'Hello, Lumpy,' and 'Hello, Pockmarka.'

Their patch-up marriage lasted until the following year, coming to a conclusive end when Burton went to a town in northern California called Oroville to make a

The 1968 movie *Boom!* showed the Burtons at their worst, in an extravagant, bad-taste production. Nothing much happened, but they strolled about in Star Trek clothes and looked decorative. *Above* Noel Coward, also in the film, has a drink with them on location, which was on Sardinia. (K)

Above Sutjeska was an odd movie, sponsored by the Yugoslav government. Burton played President Tito (here with him on the set) as a wartime guerilla. He is supposed to have been offered the part because the Yugoslavs saw him in *Where Eagles Dare*, and thought he looked like their leader when young. (S)

Below Where Eagles Dare (1969), Burton's first million-dollar movie, had him vanquishing battalions of Nazis. Here with (from left) Ingrid Pitt, Clint Eastwood and Mary Ure. (K)

Staircase (1969) starred Burton and Rex Harrison as a pair of ageing homosexuals. If they hoped, by this daring, to win Oscars, they were disappointed. Neither of these well-known heterosexuals was remotely convincing. *Left* Rex and Richard off duty. (R) (K)

Left Liz Taylor, who always fancied herself with a comb, does some unofficial hairdressing on the set of *Anne of the Thousand Days* (1969), where Burton once again found himself a King – this time Henry VIII. Geneviève Bujold as Anne Boleyn gave a satisfying performance. Burton was so bored that during one scene, shot in close-up, he left his everyday shoes and trousers on. (F) (K)

Burton was a lifelong admirer of Dylan Thomas. When *Under Milk Wood* was first broadcast, after the poet's death, Burton took the lead part that Thomas had written for himself. In 1971 Burton was in West Wales to make a film version of the play. Appearing with him were Peter O'Toole and Elizabeth Taylor. *Previous page and above and opposite* (K) (R)

Burton and Taylor were together for the television film *Divorce His...Divorce Hers* (1972).
This moment of passion sums it all up. (S)

film about the Ku Klux Klan, *The Klansman*. This marked the high, or low, point of his public rage with himself.

He began by interesting himself in an eighteen-year-old waitress at Sambo's coffee shop and buying her a $450 diamond ring because, he said, she reminded him of his daughter Kate. Elizabeth disappeared, leaving her husband to the cameras, the vodka and the press. When they asked where she was, he gave them some possibilities to choose from. 'She fell off her sandals and sprained her ankle,' he said. 'It's all black and blue and puce and other colours.' Alternatively, 'She is in Los Angeles being examined because she had an operation five months ago, and had her exquisite stomach ripped open, and they want to see if it's all better again.' Or even, 'She has gone to Hawaii to visit her brother.'

He was like someone possessed, letting words pour out of him. 'Women?' he said. 'Always think of them as my daughters. Then again, I see in women my sister when she was having a baby, and I was just a small boy. It was Christmas Eve and I thought she was dying. Which we all must do, eventually. Out of the womb, bawling, beginning our long journey to the other side. Sad, isn't it?'

His audience of reporters nodded, hoping something would happen soon, like another pretty girl he could buy a diamond for, or, better still, the return of Taylor in a temper. 'BURTON DRUNK AGAIN' wasn't much of a story. But all they were going to get was a glimpse of Burton in pain. 'Liquor helps,' he said. 'My father was a drinker, and I'm a drinker, and [his co-star in the film] Lee Marvin's a drinker. One drinks because life is big and it blinds you, it's grabbing at you from all directions all the time, and you have to tone it down. Poetry does that, too. It filters life, distils it. Poetry and drink are the greatest things on earth. Besides women. Would anybody like to hear some poetry?'

A reporter shouted, 'Tell us something about Wales.'

'Well,' said Burton obligingly, 'in Wales we subsisted mostly on trout, which we poached from a stream. We would take an enormous grand piano down and place it on the bank, and then someone would play the "Moonlight Sonata", which of course makes trout rise to the surface.' All the time he was sipping vodka. 'Then we would bash the buggers on the head with a banana. One Welshman became so stout on trout and bananas that when he died they couldn't get him out of his cottage to bury him.'

Presently the photographers moved in to take pictures. The flash bulbs popped, and Burton fell off his chair. As he picked himself up he was heard to say, 'Would you mind very much, like, just going away?'

A doctor summoned to the set declared that Burton had only weeks to live. He was whisked off to a clinic at Santa Monica, not far from where he and Sybil had stayed in their bungalow twenty-one years earlier. He was dried out and emerged looking like an old man. But he recovered; his strength hadn't deserted him.

Filmed in Hungary around the time of his wife's fortieth birthday, *Bluebeard* had Burton romping about with various attractive women including Raquel Welch. (F) (K)

Waiting for the moment when he gets an ice-pick embedded in his skull, Burton in *The Assassination of Trotsky* went from bad to worse in a pretentious picture. (R)

6

A LIFE FOR THE SAVING

THE DIVORCE from Taylor that followed ('There were too many differences,' she said. 'I have tried everything.') marked a return to calmer waters. He still drank, but not as mindlessly as before, or at least not in situations where the world was guaranteed to hear about it. He got himself involved, with Sophia Loren, in a remake for television of the classic movie, *Brief Encounter*, which invited caustic comparison with the original. But he was sober throughout the filming.

Soon he was having an affair with a woman related to the British Royal Family, Princess Elizabeth of Yugoslavia, at the time married to a merchant banker. If he missed Taylor, it was not as much as she missed him. But he remained a man ill at ease with himself. Hired to play Churchill in a television play, *A Walk with Destiny* (in America, *The Gathering Storm*), he wrote two articles attacking Churchill which were both published in the United States just before the film was transmitted. Since, earlier in his career, he had gone out of his way to say how proud he was of his acquaintance with Churchill, it seemed a strange way to behave. 'I [have] realised afresh,' Burton wrote in the *New York Times*, 'that I hate Churchill and all his kind. I hate them virulently. They have stalked down the corridors of endless power all through history.' He compared him with Attila the Hun, Genghis Khan, Hitler and Stalin, calling him a 'vindictive soldier-child' and accusing him of 'merciless ferocity.'

A clue to what was going on in Burton's head emerged a few days later, when, refusing to withdraw anything he had written, despite angry reactions, he said that 'Churchill has fascinated me from childhood – a bogeyman who hated us, the mining class, motivelessly. He ordered a few of us to be shot, you know, and the orders were carried out.' Burton was referring to events before World War I, when Churchill, then Home Secretary, sent troops to South Wales during a violent miners' strike. No one was shot – as Burton must have known – but the name of Churchill was a byword for black-hearted oppression in the mining valleys for decades afterwards, and indeed is still not forgotten there. A need to seek out his roots and reassert himself (no matter that it was at Churchill's expense) probably drove him to write as he did.

Meanwhile, Elizabeth Taylor, though busy with her own life and lovers, had no intention of abandoning Richard for good. His affair with Princess Elizabeth proceeded by fits and starts, not helped by his parallel affair with a black model who

Playing a priest for the umpteenth time, Burton went through *Exorcist II: The Heretic* (1977) like a man in a bad dream. No actor could have done much with such a misconceived film. (KY)

Below As the disillusioned psychiatrist, Martin Dysart, in the film of Peter Shaffer's *Equus* (1977). The year before, his appearance on Broadway in the stage version marked his return to public favour after his worst period of alcoholism and marital distress. (F)

had appeared in *Playboy*. When Taylor descended on him in Switzerland in the middle of 1975, a year and a bit after they were divorced, they were reconciled with tears and promises, and Burton let it be known that it was an 'indescribable feeling to know that Elizabeth is curled up in bed in the next room. That, more than anything, is what I have missed . . .'

The words had ceased to mean anything. Whatever Elizabeth Taylor may have intended or hoped for, Burton went into their revived relationship with caution and misgivings. It was at her insistence that they remarried in the African bush – or, to be precise, in a district commissioner's office in Botswana. 'My beloved is as stout as a Welsh chicken,' said Taylor, which didn't seem to help matters.

At his birthday party a week later, held in London at the Dorchester Hotel, Burton was described as being 'like a man who wasn't really there.' Even allowing for the fact that fiftieth birthdays evoke sombre thoughts, Burton seemed wretched. He drank mineral water, refused to make a speech, and left early.

A month or two later, Christmas 1975, the Burtons were staying at Gstaad when he met Susan Hunt, the wife of James Hunt, the British racing motorist. She was a discreet, middle-class young Englishwoman, no fool. To Taylor's dismay, Burton pursued the blonde and fresh-looking Mrs Hunt, already separated from her husband, with all his old vigour.

At the same time, he was preparing to go back to the stage for a season, to appear in Peter Shaffer's play *Equus* on Broadway. He had not acted in the commercial theatre for twelve years, since he did his American Hamlet. The prospect of returning to the stage excited and terrified him. There would be no director to say, 'Let's do a retake'; no film editor to achieve miracles in the cutting room. He was to play the psychiatrist, Dysart. He went for long walks on his own, in the woods, in the snow – 'thinking about Dysart, muttering Dysart, spouting Dysart.' And to help build up his self-confidence, he turned to Susan Hunt. She followed him to New York where he went to begin rehearsals in January. For the second and last time, his marriage to Taylor was coming to an end.

When the play opened in February, Burton's reviews were mixed, but there was plenty of enthusiasm, and he was treated with the respect due to a not-so-young prince who had come out of exile. The *New York Times* critic, holding out a bouquet with a knife in it, wrote that he was 'the most promising middle-aged English-speaking actor of his time.'

It was the kind of judgment that Burton would have to grin and bear for the remainder of his life. Slowly he picked up the pieces of his career and started again. Laying on the drama as usual, he said that without Susan Hunt he might very well have died. She kept him clear of destructive drinking while he was in the play.

Elizabeth Taylor wrote 'You were fantastic, love,' in lipstick on his dressing-room mirror. He was being paid $10,000 a week, but was heard grumbling how

In it for the money: Burton and Richard Harris were among the mercenaries in *The Wild Geese* (1978) a celebration of violence that went down well with audiences. Burton looked as if he enjoyed pumping bullets into the enemy, in this case black. At the time of his death he was about to start work on a sequel, *Wild Geese II*. (K)

hard it was to keep up all his houses on that kind of money. After a party, going home by limousine with Susan Hunt and others, he saw a young actress into the building where she lived, and was away long enough for Mrs Hunt to be on edge. When she chided him afterwards for being rude to her, he muttered, 'I'm bored, I'm bored.'

Still, she was good for him. Producers were still wary of his record as a drinker. It was three years since he had made a picture, and that was the ill-fated *Klansman*. He had been lucky that someone was willing to take a chance with the stage production of *Equus*. When a film version followed, Burton was far from being the inevitable choice – there had been other Dysarts in the play before he took over – but his new image, with a calmer companion to keep an eye on him, did the trick, and he was offered the part.

Finally divorced from Elizabeth and married to Susan, he ceased to make news of the old kind. He was slowing down. Always a canny self-publicist, he encouraged the belief that he was a reformed character, who would choose his films carefully in future, and do more work in the theatre. The first picture he made – between the stage and film versions of *Equus* – was an unlucky choice, a sequel to *The Exorcist* called *Exorcist II: The Heretic*. It was extraordinarily silly, and Burton, as a priest doing battle against the forces of evil, looked bewildered most of the time. His new wife (he said) told him that he must never do anything like that again, even for a million dollars. He never did, though it's unlikely that he was ever again offered a million to do anything.

After *Equus* came a couple of decent action movies, *The Medusa Touch* and *The Wild Geese*, and in 1980 he went on tour in the United States with a revival of the stage hit of two decades earlier, *Camelot*. This was well paid, highly praised and satisfying for Burton, but he found the strain too much, and before his intended year in the show was up, he had to be replaced. Cynics said it was drink again. In fact he had a chronic spinal condition that was relieved by surgery. But, as his wife Susan came to realize, Burton's addiction to drink was never far below the surface. When she gave him a present of a sports car, he drove off in it alone, and wasn't seen for hours. Police brought him home drunk. He had crashed the car, which was a write-off.

By 1982 the marriage was in trouble, and a sozzled Burton had resumed his old habit of surfacing in hotel rooms and telling the garbled story of his life to the press. His family insisted that the 'real' Richard was someone else. He was the man with a barn full of books at his house in Switzerland, the sender of large regular cheques to those he loved, the sparkling friend and joker, the reliable hero whose hallmark since adolescence had been that he was a law unto himself. He was the man who would be forgiven everything because he was Richard. But he was other things to other people: a resplendent actor with a chip on his shoulder, who

Right Perhaps glad to be out of period costume, Burton brought some excitement to his role as a gangster with homosexual tendencies in *Villain* (1971). Here with Nigel Davenport. (K)

Below For three weeks' work on *The Medusa Touch* (1978), Burton was paid half a million dollars, rather more than a dollar per second. He was a man who can make disasters happen by thinking about them, even when swathed in bandages and supposedly dead. (K)

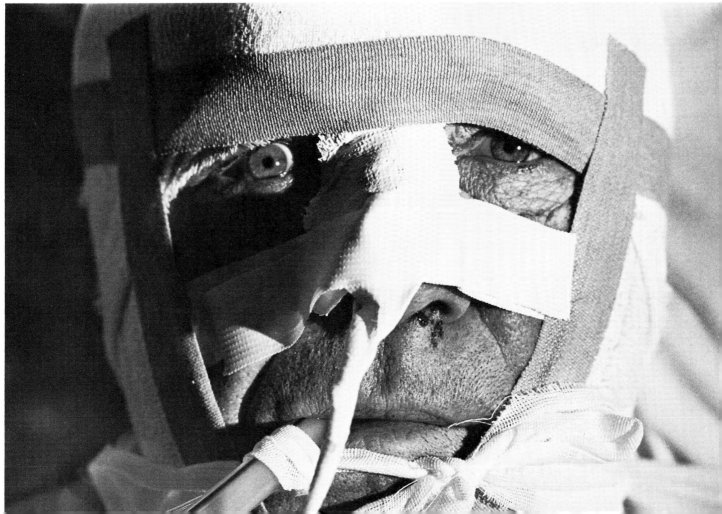

In poor health, Burton took on the gruelling role of Wagner in a nine-hour film about the composer, made in 1982. Vanessa Redgrave played his wife, Cosima. Originally intended for showing in 1983, the centenary of Wagner's death, its length caused screening problems. (S) (K) (K) (SC)

The face of *1984* – Burton as O'Brien, the sinister interrogator in the film version of Orwell's novel. This was his last major role. (PA)

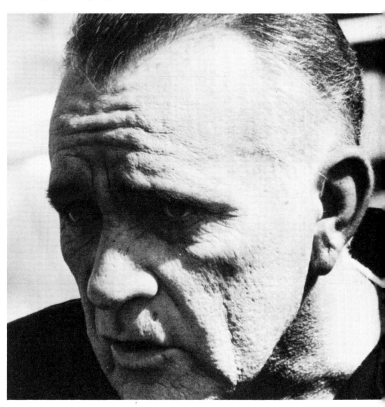

couldn't or wouldn't take his profession seriously; an obsessive lover with an unslakeable thirst; a melancholic Welshman who might have been content with the lower profile of a writer, give or take a couple of genes.

'Susan?' he said to the waiting pencils. 'Taller than a ghost, and just as remote, I may say. She is so English, so hopelessly remote. Oh God, don't put all that down. Elizabeth, oh so totally different. I might run from her for a thousand years, and she from me for a thousand years, and she is still my baby child. We are inexorably bound . . .'

But Taylor was for talking about, even for appearing with in a New York stage revival of *Private Lives*: not for living with. After more alcoholic episodes, Burton, in Vienna to play Wagner in a very long film about the composer, found a new companion in the shape of Sally Hay, a BBC production assistant. They were married the following year, 1983. Like her predecessor, she was said to have saved Burton's life. Perhaps it was true: by now he was a man who needed a lot of saving. Despite the damage to his health, he seemed as busy as ever in 1984, working on a feature film of Orwell's book, *1984*, on an American television series, *Ellis Island*, and, in early August, preparing for a new adventure movie, *Wild Geese II*. On Sunday 5 August, at home in Switzerland with his wife, he had a stroke, a brain haemorrhage, and died later that day. His father, also an alcoholic, had died of the same condition, though at a greater age.

Richard Burton was only fifty-eight. At least the fifty-odd films that he made – good, bad and indifferent – ensure that something of his qualities will survive. The eyes stare out of a complex face. Buried in a Swiss grave four days later, a copy of the *Collected Poems* of Dylan Thomas went with him. His daughter Kate read, in a clear American accent,

> *Do not go gentle into that good night.*
> *Rage, rage against the dying of the light . . .*

Richard Burton liked to lavish jewels on Elizabeth Taylor almost as much as she liked to have them lavished on her. (R)

In 1983, Burton and Taylor came together again on the Broadway stage in a revival of Noel Coward's *Private Lives*. Crowds went to see it; the critics were cool. The weekend this picture was taken, Burton went off to Mexico and married Sally Hay. (SC)

Right Richard and Elizabeth dressed to kill. (S)

Snowballs. (R)

Left Together. (S)

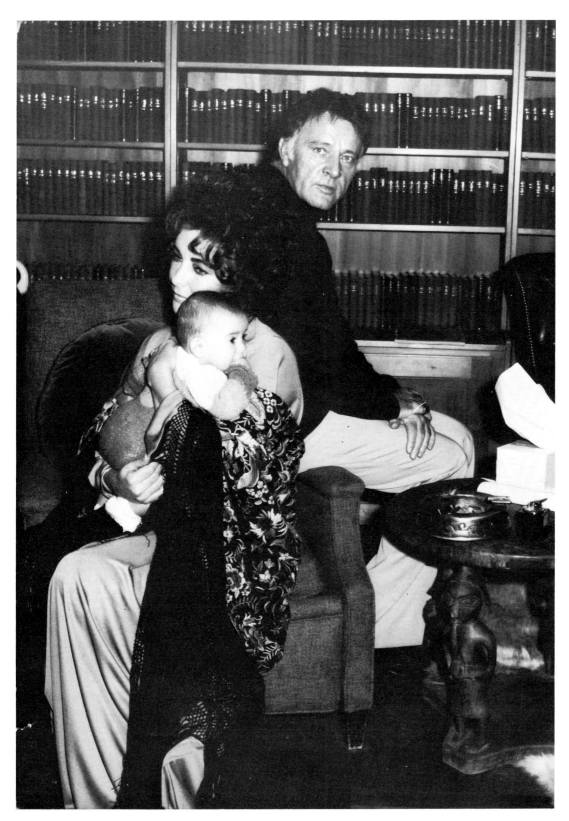

With Elizabeth Taylor and her grandchild. (RB)

People came to associate an opulent life-style with the Burtons. In the league of the world's super-rich they were only modest members. But the publicity they attracted meant that they always seemed to be splashing their money around on private planes, large cars and yachts. (S)

Below Faces in the crowd: the Burtons never found it easy to go anywhere unnoticed. But with the fight between Henry Cooper and Cassius Clay (as he then was) going on, the audience had something else to look at. (S)

Above Enjoying the good life on the yacht of their friend Aristotle Onassis. (R)

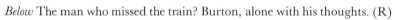

Below The man who missed the train? Burton, alone with his thoughts. (R)

Below With his daughter Kate (left) and wife Sally. Burton and Kate were filming in an American TV series, *Ellis Island*. *Right* A scene from the film. (S)

Left With his third wife Susan, formerly married to the racing driver, James Hunt, in 1980. 'Taller than a ghost, and just as remote', Burton said of her, after they parted a year or two later. (S)

Below The newly married Richard Burton and Sally Hay (left) celebrate Elizabeth's engagement to a Mexican lawyer, Victor Luna, intended to be husband number 8. Burton and Taylor were appearing in *Private Lives* at the time, August 1983. (SC)

Above Filming *The Wild Geese* with his old friend Roger Moore, whose 50th birthday called for this celebration. From left – Susan and Richard Burton, Luisa and Roger Moore, Hardy Kruger and friend. (S)

Right Another Elizabeth – Princess Elizabeth of Yugoslavia – was one of Burton's companions in 1974, after his first divorce from Miss Taylor, and before they remarried. (KY)

RICHARD BURTON ON THE STAGE

The Druid's Rest (Emlyn Williams) London, 1944
Measure for Measure (William Shakespeare) Oxford, 1944
Castle Anna (adapted from the novel by Elizabeth Bowen) London, 1948
Dark Summer, 1948
Captain Brassbound's Conversion (George Bernard Shaw), 1949
The Lady's Not For Burning (Christopher Fry) London, 1949
The Boy With a Cart (Christopher Fry) London, New York, 1950
Henry IV Part I and II (William Shakespeare) Stratford, 1951
Henry V (William Shakespeare) Stratford, 1951
The Tempest (William Shakespeare) Stratford, 1951
Legend of Lovers (Jean Anouilh) New York, 1951
Montserrat (Lillian Hellman) London, 1952
Hamlet (William Shakespeare) London, 1953–4
Twelfth Night (William Shakespeare) London, 1953–4
King John (William Shakespeare) London, 1953–4
Coriolanus (William Shakespeare) London, 1953–4
The Tempest (William Shakespeare) London, 1953–4
Henry V (William Shakespeare) London, 1955–6
Othello (William Shakespeare) London, 1956
Time Remembered (Jean Anouilh) New York, 1957–8
Camelot, New York, 1960
Hamlet (William Shakespeare) USA, 1964
Dr Faustus (Christopher Marlowe) Oxford, 1966
Equus (Peter Shaffer) New York, 1976
Camelot, USA, 1980–1
Private Lives (Noël Coward) USA, 1983

RICHARD BURTON'S FILMS

The Last Days of Dolwyn, 1948
Now Barabbas Was a Robber, 1949
Waterfront, 1950
The Woman With No Name, 1951
Green Grow the Rushes, 1951
My Cousin Rachel, 1952
The Desert Rats, 1953
The Robe, 1953
The Prince of Players, 1955
The Rains of Ranchipur, 1955
Alexander the Great, 1956
Sea Wife, 1957
Bitter Victory, 1957
Look Back in Anger, 1959
The Bramble Bush, 1960
Ice Palace, 1960
The Longest Day, 1962
Cleopatra, 1963
The VIPs, 1963
Becket, 1964
The Night of the Iguana, 1964
Hamlet, 1964
The Sandpiper, 1965
What's New Pussycat? 1965
The Spy Who Came In from the Cold, 1966
Who's Afraid of Virginia Woolf? 1966

The Taming of the Shrew, 1967
The Comedians, 1967
Dr Faustus, 1968
Boom!, 1968
Candy, 1968
Where Eagles Dare, 1969
Staircase, 1969
Anne of the Thousand Days, 1969
Villain, 1971
Raid on Rommel, 1971
Under Milk Wood, 1971
Hammersmith Is Out, 1972
The Assassination of Trotsky, 1972
Sutjeska, 1972
Bluebeard, 1972
Repressaglia – Massacre in Rome, 1973
The Voyage, 1974
The Klansman, 1974
Exorcist II: The Heretic, 1977
Equus, 1977
The Medusa Touch, 1978
The Wild Geese, 1978
Breakthrough (Sgt. Steiner), 1978
Circle of Two, 1982
Wagner, 1984
1984, 1984

ISBN 0 297 78564 8 (cased)
ISBN 0 297 78565 6 (paperback)

Picture Research by Tomás Graves

Designed by Kevin Shenton, assisted by Joy FitzSimmons for
George Weidenfeld and Nicolson
91 Clapham High Street
London sw4 7TA

Printed in Great Britain by
Butler & Tanner Ltd, Frome and London